THEODORE
THE RUNAWAY HAMSTER

To Emily and Jeremy

In memory of Theodore and all the runaway pets

Text copyright © 2018 by Linda Franks
Illustrations copyright © 2018 by Thomas Rhodes

Colored and Designed by Bridget Rhodes
RhoRho Illustrations (www.rhorho.co.uk)

First Published in the USA 2018

All rights reserved. This book or any portion thereof may not be reproduced or used in any manner whatsoever without the express written permission of the author except for the use of brief quotations in a book review.

First printing, 2018

ISBN 13: 978-1987454864
ISBN 10: 1987454863

100% of the profits from this book go to the charity organization AKUN in Anchorage, AK, USA.
www.supportakun.org

10 9 8 7 6 5 4 3 2 1

THEODORE
THE RUNAWAY HAMSTER

by Linda Franks
illustrated by Thomas Rhodes

A few weeks ago, Emily got a baby hamster. He was just a tiny ball of fur.

Every day, when she came back home, she dropped her school bag and ran to the cage to check on Theodore the hamster.

Emily loved her new pet.
He was so cute and fluffy!

After school, they played together and for both of them, it was their favorite time of the day.

As Theodore the hamster grew up, he became a VERY clever pet.

He knew his name and when called, he would run towards Emily.

He could also get treats out of tricky-to-open snack boxes.

There was nothing he could not do to grab these tasty bites!

Every morning before going to school, Emily would make sure that Theodore the hamster had all he needed for the day: a clean cage, food and water.

But little did she know that he had worked out how to open the door!

One day, Emily came back from school and ran to the cage as usual.
Only this time, she found it empty.

THEODORE THE HAMSTER WAS GONE!

Had she left the door unlocked by mistake?

Had Theodore managed to open the door himself?

The little handle was all chewed up.

Emily called his name and looked everywhere but Theodore the hamster was nowhere to be seen.

Was he in a drawer?

Maybe...

...under a bed?

Or perhaps behind books?

After thinking for a while, Emily had a great idea: she sprinkled some of Theodore's favorite treats near the door of the cage and waited patiently to see if he would return.

After waiting for what felt like a very long time,

Emily's plan worked.

Theodore was back!

A few weeks later, when Emily came back from school, she found out that Theodore had run away again.
It was now the fourth escapade and she was worried that maybe he did not like being in his cage.

As usual, she left treats near the cage and listened carefully for the sound of her pet's little feet on the floor.

And she waited,

and waited,

...and waited even longer!

But this time,
Theodore did not come back.
The treats were still there the day after and Emily was very worried.

"Where can he be?"
She thought.

"Is he hungry?"

"Is he lost and scared?"

Two more days went by, and there was still no sign of Theodore the hamster. Emily missed him so much!
The house felt empty without her furry little friend.

Would he ever come back?

Emily looked for ways to stop herself from worrying about her missing pet.

So she decided to practice her piano for a while.

After playing her favorite tune, Emily noticed that something was not quite right with the piano: some keys were making a weird sound.

Emily's mum came to help investigate.

The two of them opened the top of the piano to see what was wrong with the keys.

They quickly discovered what the problem was: the piece of felt inside had been chewed up.

"How strange!" said Emily's mum.

"Could we have mice in our house?"

And very soon, in the bottom part of the piano, they found a surprise:

"Oh, look who is here!"

Curled up and sleeping peacefully in a soft bed of felt was...

THEODORE

THE RUNAWAY HAMSTER!

Printed in Great Britain
by Amazon